I Can See

In My Backyard

By Czeena Devera

2 I see a tree in my backyard.

I see a nest in my backyard.

3

4 I see a garden in my backyard.

I see a dandelion in my backyard. 5

6 I see a ladybug in my backyard.

I see a tree house in my backyard.

8 I see a hammock in my backyard.

I see a fort in my backyard.

10 I see a swing in my backyard.

I see a pool in my backyard.

I see a trampoline in my backyard.

I see family in my backyard.

Word List

backyard	ladybug	pool
tree	house	trampoline
nest	hammock	family
garden	fort	
dandelion	swing	

I see a tree in my backyard.

I see a nest in my backyard.

I see a garden in my backyard.

I see a dandelion in my backyard.

I see a ladybug in my backyard.

I see a tree house in my backyard.

I see a hammock in my backyard.

I see a fort in my backyard.

I see a swing in my backyard.

I see a pool in my backyard.

I see a trampoline in my backyard.

I see family in my backyard.

Published in the United States of America by Cherry Lake Publishing
Ann Arbor, Michigan
www.cherrylakepublishing.com

Photo Credits: © malerapaso/iStockphoto, front cover, 1, 15; © irin-k/Shutterstock.com, back cover, 6; © Artazum/
Shutterstock.com, 2; © Oldrich/Shutterstock.com, 3; © Elena Elisseeva/Shutterstock.com, 4; © Flynt/Dreamstime.
com, 5; © Cebas/iStockphoto, 7; © InnaFelker/iStockphoto, 8; © Mark Herreid/Shutterstock.com, 9; © Cheryl-
Annette Parker/Shutterstock.com, 10; © KatarzynaBialasiewicz/iStockphoto, 11; © nnattalli/Shutterstock.com, 12;
© monkeybusinessimages/iStockphoto, 13

Cherry Blossom Press is an imprint of Cherry Lake Publishing.

Library of Congress Cataloging-in-Publication Data

Names: Devera, Czeena, author.
Title: In my backyard / Czeena Devera.
Description: Ann Arbor, MI : Cherry Lake Publishing, 2019. | Series: I can see |
    Includes bibliographical references and index. | Audience: Pre-school, excluding Kindergarten.
Identifiers: LCCN 2018034492 | ISBN 9781534140370 (pdf) | ISBN 9781534139176 (pbk.) |
    ISBN 9781534141575 (hosted ebook)
Subjects: LCSH: Plants—Juvenile literature. | Outdoor recreation—Juvenile literature. | Reading (Preschool)
Classification: LCC QK49 .D44 2019 | DDC 581—dc23
LC record available at https://lccn.loc.gov/2018034492

Printed in the United States of America
Corporate Graphics

CHERRY BLOSSOM PRESS